MY DREAM MAP

MY DREAM MAP

An Interactive Companion to
Put Your Dream to the Test

JOHN C. MAXWELL

THOMAS NELSON
Since 1798

NASHVILLE DALLAS MEXICO CITY RIO DE JANEIRO BEIJING

Published in Nashville, Tennessee, by Thomas Nelson. Thomas Nelson is a registered trademark of Thomas Nelson, Inc.

Published in association with Yates & Yates, www.yates2.com.

Page design by Mandi Cofer.

Thomas Nelson, Inc., titles may be purchased in bulk for educational, business, fund-raising, or sales promotional use. For information, please e-mail Special Markets@ThomasNelson.com.

ISBN 978-1-4002-8074-2 (IE)

Library of Congress Cataloging-in-Publication Data

Maxwell, John C., 1947–
    My dream map : an interactive companion to put your dream to the test / John C. Maxwell.
      p. cm.
    Includes bibliographical references.
    ISBN 978-1-4002-0256-0
    1. Motivation (Psychology) 2. Success. I. Title.
    BF503.M385 2009
    158—dc22
                                    2008054603

Printed in the United States of America

09 10 11 12 13 QW 9 8 7 6 5 4 3

CONTENTS

Contents

ACKNOWLEDGMENTS

Thank you to Charlie Wetzel, my writer, for his assistance with this book in developing a process that will help others create a map for their dreams.

CREATING A MAP FOR YOUR DREAM

I've been writing books and teaching at conferences for more than thirty years, and one of the things I've discovered is that many people can have a difficult time taking general concepts and applying them to their specific lives. It's not because of lack of intelligence or desire. It's just that examining themselves and putting principles into practice can be daunting. That's one reason I've included application exercises in most of my books.

At the same time, I don't want to bog down people in numerous activities that take too much time. My advice to people who read my books is generally to use the application exercises if they help, but to skip them if they can easily figure out how to apply the concepts to their lives on their own.

But what if you really *want* to dig in and do substantial work to apply what you're learning from a book? How do you take the learning process to the next level? What if you would like to delve deeper into the process of discovering your dream while reading *Put Your Dream to the Test*?

My Dream Map is my answer to that question.

A dream is an especially difficult thing to describe. Dreams aren't concrete until they come to pass. Before then, they are like clouds. When both of us look at a cloud, you may see one thing while I see another. And the picture you see in one moment may quickly change when the first wind comes along. As time goes by—a day, a week, or a year—you may not even remember what you once saw. That's why I offer this book as a way to make your dream more concrete. Let's face it: when it comes to giving voice and life to their dreams, most people need some help.

When I got the idea for writing *Put Your Dream to the Test*, I almost didn't move forward with it because of the nebulous quality of dreams. I had seen too many speakers and authors talk about dreams using what I considered to be smoke and mirrors, making claims such as, "If you can dream it, you can achieve it." Not true! I've dreamed about winning an NBA championship, but I guarantee it's never going to happen!

This book is designed to help you discover and define your dream. My desire is to help you draw a map that you can then use to achieve what you were created to do. If you want to really dig down—or if you want to help someone else do it—then this book will help. To create your dream map, you will need to answer some questions. You will have to spend time thinking and journaling. You will need to talk to people. If you're a person of faith, you should devote time to prayer.

Start by taking the Dream Test that begins on page 1. Read *Put Your Dream to the Test* (either straight through or a chapter at a time). Then work your way though this book. There are ten sections, one for each of the ten questions found in *Put Your Dream to the Test*. The bottom line is that you will have to engage in a process.

How long will that take? That depends on you. The amount of time will be affected by how self-aware you are, how honest you are about your strengths and weaknesses, your history, and how much time and energy you've already given to the subject in the past. But isn't your dream worth it? Trust me, the time you spend will be an investment in yourself. Taking several weeks or months to greatly increase the odds of your success will be well worth the effort. Nobody wanders his or her way to a dream, and nobody achieves a dream by accident. Don't short-cut the process and risk cheating yourself out of your dream!

So, are you ready to give it your best shot? Are you willing to do the hard, lonely, inglorious work that's necessary for achieving a dream? Remember, all's well that begins well. You can discover your dream. And you can actually live it.

THE DREAM TEST

The first step in creating a useful map is knowing your starting point. Take the following test to help you make that assessment. Think of it as a way of writing "You Are Here" on your dream map.

For each statement below, please respond by writing the number that best represents your current life (not where others think you should be, where you wish you were, or where you hope to be someday):

0—No

1—Somewhat

2—Yes

1. The Ownership Question: Is my dream really my dream?

A. I would be the person in the world most pleased if I accomplished my dream.

B. I have publicly shared my dream with other people, including those I love.

C. My dream has been challenged by others, and I still embrace it.

D. As I've gotten older, I have become more certain that my dream is really mine.

E. I believe that my dream is in alignment with the purpose of my life.

Score for This Section _____

2. The Clarity Question: Do I clearly see my dream?

 A. I can explain the main gist of my dream in a single sentence.

 B. I have spent many hours defining my dream in great detail.

 C. I have written a clear description of my dream that includes its main features or objectives.

 D. I could answer nearly any question about the *what* (if not the *how*) of my dream.

 E. I have revised and written my dream more than once.

Score for This Section _____

3. The Reality Question: Am I depending on factors within my control to achieve my dream?

 A. I know what my greatest strengths and talents are, and my dream relies heavily on them.

 B. My current habits and daily practices strongly contribute to the potential success of my dream.

 C. I expect the realization of my dream to be one of the most difficult things I'll ever do.

 D. My dream is likely to come true even if I am unlucky, if important people ignore or oppose me, or if I encounter serious obstacles.

 E. I am willing to pay any and every price needed to achieve my dream as long as it doesn't violate my personal values.

Score for This Section _____

4. The Passion Question: Does my dream compel me to follow it?

 A. I can think of nothing I would rather do more than see my dream fulfilled.

 B. I think about my dream every day and often wake up or fall asleep thinking about it.

C. Even if I believed I could not completely fulfill my dream, I would still be excited about the pursuit of it.

D. This dream has been consistently important to me for at least a year.

E. When it comes to my dream, I display more initiative than I do in any other part of my life.

Score for This Section _____

5. The Pathway Question: Do I have a strategy to reach my dream?

A. I have written a strategic plan for how I intend to accomplish my dream.

B. I have made a realistic assessment of where I'm starting from and how far I must go to achieve my dream.

C. I have identified all the resources available to me and have incorporated them as part of my strategy.

D. I have set concrete monthly and yearly goals as part of my plan.

E. I have shared my plan with three people I respect to get their feedback.

Score for This Section _____

6. The People Question: Have I included the people I need to realize my dream?

A. I frequently spend time with people who inspire me.

B. I have surrounded myself with people who are honest with me about my strengths and weaknesses.

C. I have recruited people with complementary skills to help me accomplish my dream.

D. I have found a way to express my dream to others in a way that connects logically, emotionally, and visually.

E. I work at transferring the vision by frequently casting it with my people clearly and creatively.

Score for This Section _____

7. The Cost Question: Am I willing to pay the price for my dream?

A. I can recount specific costs I have already paid toward achieving my dream.

B. I have already considered what I am willing to trade next to achieve my dream.

C. I am willing to face fierce criticism from others as I pursue my dream because I know it's right for me.

D. My mind-set is that I will *never* arrive at a time or place where I will no longer have to keep paying for my dream.

E. No matter what, I will not compromise my values, ruin my health, or damage my family to pursue my dream.

Score for This Section _____

8. The Tenacity Question: Am I moving closer to my dream?

A. I can identify obstacles I have already overcome in the pursuit of my dream.

B. I possess an attitude of initiative related to my dream, and I am unafraid of taking bold steps to take me closer to my dream.

C. I do something every day—even if it's very small—to move closer to my dream.

D. I expect to do extraordinarily difficult things to grow and change so that I can accomplish my dream, and I have prepared myself mentally to do them.

E. I refuse to take no for an answer when it comes to my dream.

Score for This Section _____

9. The Fulfillment Question: Does working toward my dream bring satisfaction?

A. I am willing to give up my idealism in order to make my dream become reality.

B. I understand that the pursuit of any significant dream leads one into a difficult learning curve, and I am ready to cheerfully face it.

C. I am ready and willing to work for years or even decades to achieve my dream because it is that important to me.

D. I have made it my goal to make discoveries about myself and the world "on the way" to my dream because I know that will help sustain me.

E. I enjoy the pursuit of my dream so much that even if I fail, I will consider my life to have been well spent.

Score for This Section _____

10. The Significance Question: Does my dream benefit others?

A. I can honestly say that pursuit of my dream allows me to be engaged in a cause greater than myself.

B. I can name specific people other than myself who will benefit if my dream is realized.

C. Even if the entire dream is not accomplished, others will be helped along the way.

D. I am working to build a team of like-minded people to accomplish my dream.

E. What I'm doing to achieve my dream will matter in five, twenty, or one hundred years.

Score for This Section _____

Total Score _____

Key

Add your scores for each section, and then calculate your total score. Use the key below to see where you stand.

91–100	You are well on your way; the odds are very high that you will achieve your dream.
81–90	You need to do some work, but you are headed in the right direction for achieving your dream.
71–80	You need to make significant changes if you want to achieve your dream.
70 or Below	You have a long way to go; achieving your dream will require significant rethinking and major changes in the way you live.

CHAPTER 1

The Ownership Question
Is My Dream Really My Dream?

Everybody has to start somewhere. Even the greatest dreams, the most earth-shaking achievements, began as a mere concept, an idea in the mind of some individual.

What makes a dream worthy? It has to be yours. The achievability of a dream doesn't depend primarily on its size or scope, nor does it rely on the individual dreamer's talent as much as it does on that person's ownership of it. Show me a dream achieved and I'll show you a dreamer who owned it—heart and soul. You have a chance of getting where you want to go only if you truly own your dream.

YOU ARE HERE

What was your score for the ownership section of the Dream Test? That number (out of a possible 10) represents your level of ownership for your dream. What is your reaction to that? Take some time to reflect on it, and write about what it means as your starting point.

SURVEYING THE TERRAIN

Write a first draft of your dream. You don't need to make it pretty or perfect—just get the basic idea down on paper and be as specific as you can be.

ASKING FOR DIRECTIONS

While you are working your way through the dream questions and creating your dream map, one of the things you will be asked to do is to talk with people who are far ahead of you in the journey. If I had to point to a single action most responsible for my success, especially early in my career, it would be interviewing successful people so that I could learn from them. I strongly recommend that you follow through with my suggestions concerning interviews. If you do, by the time you've gone through every chapter of *My Dream Map,* you will have interviewed ten or more people whose achievements you highly respect.

For the Ownership Question, make an appointment with someone who has accomplished a dream. Write here the questions you will ask. Be sure to ask questions regarding his ownership of the dream, especially during the early stages of his journey. Take notes on his answers in the space provided.

My Dream Map

GIVING LIFE TO THE MAP

Start reading a biography of someone who accomplished a dream in an area similar to yours. (You may want to make reading biographies a regular practice in the coming year.) Record important observations from what you read here.

JOURNALING

Spend the next several days or weeks wrestling through the ownership issue. Make sure that as you reflect and write, you answer the following questions:

- [ ] Why do you want to accomplish this dream?
- [ ] Why are *you* the right person for this dream, and why is this dream right for you?
- [ ] What specific talents, strengths, and personality traits will help you achieve this dream?
- [ ] What kind of research have you done on your dream?
- [ ] What is your earliest recollection of knowing you wanted to achieve this dream?
- [ ] Does anyone else in your life or personal history also share this dream for you? If so, who would be happier if you achieved this dream—you or the other people? (Note: If you answer that some other person would be happier, that is a red flag. Your dream very well may not be *your* dream.)
- [ ] What would happen to you if you were not able to pursue this dream?
- [ ] What would happen to you if you pursued it and failed to achieve it?
- [ ] What would change in your life if you accomplished this dream?

My Dream Map

My Dream Map

My Dream Map

My Dream Map

_____

_____

_____

_____

_____

_____

_____

_____

_____

_____

_____

_____

_____

_____

_____

_____

_____

_____

_____

OBSERVATIONS AND CONCLUSIONS

What have you learned about yourself, your dream, and the ownership issue from journaling?

_____

_____

_____

_____

_____

_____

_____

_____

_____

_____

_____

_____

_____

PLOTTING YOUR COURSE

What must you change in order to take yourself to a 10 in the area of ownership? Write it down, and integrate it into your calendar and daily work habits.

CHAPTER 2

The Clarity Question
Do I Clearly See My Dream?

There are people who say, "If you can see it, you can seize it." That's not always true. However, what is true is that if you *cannot* see it, you *will not* seize it. You will be able to achieve a dream only if you can see it clearly!

Bringing clarity to the dream can be very difficult and time consuming. This section of *My Dream Map* may take you the longest to complete. That's okay. Accomplishing your dream may take you many years. Taking days, weeks, or even months to clarify it first won't slow you down. It will actually speed you toward your dream. You cannot reach an uncertain destination. Besides, if you allow your dream to remain fuzzy and undefined, you won't be able to do much of the other work that is necessary to make it become a reality. If a dream is worth doing, it's worth defining. Take the time now to make it clear.

YOU ARE HERE

What was your score for the clarity section of the Dream Test? That number (out of a possible 10) represents how clear your dream is to you. Do you think your score on the test was fair and representative of your dream's clarity? If your score was lower than 9, then write about why you think you lack clarity.

SURVEYING THE TERRAIN

It's time to take the vision of your dream to the next level. Describe your dream in as much detail as possible. Think big, but also be specific. Paint a picture using words. Use numbers if appropriate. Describe what the achievement of your dream looks like. Describe how it makes you feel. Capture as much of the scope, texture, and detail as possible.

ASKING FOR DIRECTIONS

For the Clarity Question, make an appointment with a person who has accomplished a dream that you consider to have been nearly impossible. Write here the questions you will ask, paying particular attention to how clear the dream was to her before it was realized. Ask her if she had any special way of keeping the vision for the dream in view. Take notes on her answers in the space provided.

My Dream Map

GIVING LIFE TO THE MAP

Think about the most audacious dreams that have been accomplished in human history. Which stands out to you as the most remarkable or interesting? Spend some time doing research about the person who had the dream and brought it to fruition. Pay particular attention to when the dream became clear to him or her and how that affected the process of achieving it. Record your observations here.

JOURNALING

Spend the next several weeks thinking about your dream and giving it as much detail as you can. As you reflect and write, make sure you answer the following questions:

- ☐ Does your dream make the most of your circumstances and opportunities?
- ☐ What are your emotions telling you about your dream? Is it on target?
- ☐ What does your intuition tell you about the rightness of your dream?
- ☐ How does your dream align with your life purpose?
- ☐ If it doesn't, how can you adjust your dream so that there is alignment?
- ☐ Do your unique life experiences come into play in the creation of your dream?
- ☐ Have you allowed the things that inspire you—music, books, movies, memories, photographs, quotes, and so on—to contribute positively to the creation of your dream?
- ☐ Have you talked to other people who have accomplished similar dreams?
- ☐ If not, can you find a way to do that?
- ☐ How can you add more detail to your picture of the dream?

My Dream Map

My Dream Map

My Dream Map

OBSERVATIONS AND CONCLUSIONS

What have you learned about yourself, your dream, and the Clarity Question from journaling?

PLOTTING YOUR COURSE

Now that you have spent time journaling, talked to successful people, and done some research, it's time to rewrite your dream. Though this may seem tedious, do not skip this step! Your goal is to express your dream on the following pages in two different ways:

First, describe it in great detail with specific goals or objectives, similar to the way that Mike Hyatt did. (Reread "The Clarity Question" in *Put Your Dream to the Test* if needed.)

Second, describe your dream in a single concise sentence that you can easily write on the back of a business card. The idea is that if you were on an elevator and your hero got on and asked you your dream, you would be able to state it before the elevator reached its destination.

After doing these two things, put a written copy of your dream someplace where you will see it every day.

My Dream Map

My Dream Map

CHAPTER 3

The Reality Question
Am I Depending on Factors Within
My Control to Achieve My Dream?

People who accomplish great things are both dreamers and realists. They see and own a vision that may be unbelievable to everyone in the world but them. At the same time, they find a way to deal with the reality of who and where they are, looking the facts straight in the eye without blinking.

This part of *My Dream Map* will require you to take a hard look at yourself. You will need to honestly assess not only your personal strengths, but also where you currently fall short. You cannot ignore reality and achieve your dream. However, you cannot allow reality to discourage you if your dream is the right one for you. It's a fine line to walk, but it's a skill you must acquire to get where you ultimately want to go.

YOU ARE HERE

What was your score for the reality section of the Dream Test? That number (out of a possible 10) represents how realistic you currently are when it comes to your dream. If your score was high, you may not have very much work to do. If it was especially low, you will need to engage in a development process that will probably take time. This chapter will merely be your starting point, but that's okay. Hard work is part of the reality of achieving a dream.

In writing, explain the place you are starting from in the pursuit of your dream, and describe the gap that you see between where you are and where you want to be. What obstacles do you expect to have to overcome to get where you want to go?

SURVEYING THE TERRAIN

The first step in facing reality is assessing your strengths and weaknesses. If you haven't done that in the last two years (or if you have never done it), do it now. I highly recommend that you start with StrengthsFinder and a personality test such as Myers-Briggs or DISC. If your dream requires leadership, take the 21 Laws Leadership Evaluation, which you can find in the revised and updated version of *The 21 Irrefutable Laws of Leadership*. If you are a Christian, I recommend that you take a spiritual gifts test. If your dream is related to your profession and there are assessments or evaluations available related to it, take them. You get the idea. Don't rule out anything that may help you.

Once you have done some exploring in this area, write a summary of yourself incorporating all of the information. Be sure to identify your top three to seven strengths, and make note of the areas where you are weakest.

ASKING FOR DIRECTIONS

Contact the most accomplished person in your circle of acquaintances who knows you and your work well. Ask the individual to assess your strengths and weaknesses. Give the person the following questions far enough ahead of time before you meet so that he can think about the answers.

1. What have you observed to be my greatest strengths (name at least three)?
2. In what areas do you think I have been most productive?
3. What skill or talent makes me unique in my ability to achieve success either personally or professionally?
4. If I had to narrow my focus to just one area in the future, which one would you say has the greatest potential?
5. In what ways do I add value to other people?
6. In what ways do you think I need to improve when working with people?
7. What are my greatest weaknesses (name three)?
8. Do you think any of those weaknesses could derail my career or personal life?
9. On a scale of 1 to 10 (with 10 being the highest), how tenacious have I been to learn and grow?
10. What one piece of advice would you give me that would most help me to achieve my dream?

When you meet, review each question and then listen to the person's answers. If you need more clarification about some of the answers he gives you, you may ask follow-up questions. However, you are not to defend yourself or give excuses for your past actions. Otherwise, you may not get honest feedback. If you are a highly emotional person, during the interview pretend you are playing poker and you don't want the person you're interviewing to know what you are thinking and feeling. The point is to *listen and learn*.

Take notes on the answers in the space provided. If you feel that you haven't received enough information or accurate information, schedule meetings with other people, and repeat the process.

My Dream Map

_____

_____

_____

_____

_____

_____

_____

_____

_____

_____

_____

_____

_____

_____

_____

_____

_____

_____

My Dream Map

GIVING LIFE TO THE MAP

One secret of successful people is that they build upon their strengths. The older they get, the more focused they become. (Early in my career, it felt as if I did everything. Today in my professional life, I do only four things: communicate, create, network, and lead.)

To close the gap between who you are now and who you must become to achieve your dream, you must create and follow a personal growth plan. Start by identifying your top five strengths. Next, describe how these strengths relate to the achievement of your dream. Note whether there are any weaknesses in your abilities that would be difficult or impossible to strengthen. If there are, you will need to address them when you work on the People Question by finding others to complement your strengths

Now, in the space below create a one-year growth plan for building on the five strengths. In the coming year, read two books related to each strength. Plan one interview with an expert in your number one strength. Listen to one podcast or lesson on CD every week related to any of your top five strengths.

You'll notice that your growth plan is always to be focused on your strengths. However, there is one exception to this rule. Character flaws can prevent you from achieving success. If one of the weaknesses that you identified during this discovery process was related to character, you need to find and enlist a mentor to help you work through the issue. You cannot successfully tackle character issues on your own.

My Dream Map

JOURNALING

Spend the next several days or weeks working through the reality issue. Make sure that as you reflect and write, you answer the following questions:

- ☐ What are the qualities needed in a person who desires to accomplish your dream?
- ☐ What background and what kinds of experiences does that kind of person usually possess?
- ☐ What skills do you need to acquire to be able to bridge the gap to your dream?
- ☐ How long will it take you to acquire those skills?
- ☐ What will it cost you to possess those experiences and acquire those skills?
- ☐ What habits must you begin cultivating today in order to become someone who can achieve this dream?
- ☐ Do people whom you respect affirm that you either are or have the potential to become someone who can achieve this dream?
- ☐ What do you expect to be the greatest obstacle you will face while working to achieve your dream?
- ☐ How long do you expect the accomplishment of your dream to take?
- ☐ How much work will it require?

My Dream Map

My Dream Map

OBSERVATIONS AND CONCLUSIONS

What have you learned about yourself, your dream, and the reality issue from journaling? What habits do you need to cultivate to develop into someone who can accomplish your dream? Write them here.

PLOTTING YOUR COURSE

Now that you've worked on discovering your strengths and spent time reflecting and journaling, reconfirm that your growth plan is on track. If it is, schedule it in your calendar for the next year.

It's also time to plan how to work on cultivating habits that will help you become successful. Identify five or six habits that you need to develop. Work on each habit on a daily basis for at least sixty days.

CHAPTER 4

The Passion Question
Does My Dream Compel Me to Follow It?

Passion is the fuel that gives successful people the energy needed to keep pursuing their dreams. Without a large measure of passion, there would be few advances in science, medicine, the arts, technology, or personal achievement.

Passion can be difficult to measure. You can probably recognize passion when you see it. But how do you quantify it? How do you measure your level of passion? Maybe even more important, how do you increase it if it's not high enough? Difficult as that may be, these are the tasks you are being asked to tackle.

YOU ARE HERE

What was your score for the passion section of the Dream Test? That number (out of a possible 10) represents how passionate you currently are when it comes to your dream. Another way to judge your passion is to use the Passion Scale that was in *Put Your Dream to the Test*. I've included it below. Think about your dream, and then gauge how passionate you are about it using this scale:

10. My passion is so hot that it sets other people on fire.
9. I cannot imagine my life without my dream.
8. I willingly sacrifice other important things for it.
7. I am fired up by it and often preoccupied with it.
6. I enjoy it as one of many interests.
5. I can take it or leave it.
4. I prefer not to think about it.
3. I go out of my way to avoid it.
2. I've put it on my list of least favorite things.
1. I would rather have a root canal without anesthesia.

If your score is low (below an 8), you need to work to increase your passion. If it's already high, your goal should be to sustain your passion.

SURVEYING THE TERRAIN

Where does passion come from? It comes from within, but what produces it? First of all, having passion is a choice. You must *choose* to be a passionate person. That is especially important if your personality is reserved or at all perfectionistic. Second, passion rises in people who are able to tap into the things that really matter to them.

Take some time to reflect on the following things:

* What makes you sing (gives you joy)?
* What makes you cry (touches your heart)?
* What makes you go (energizes you)?

Write about those things here.

_____

_____

_____

_____

_____

_____

_____

My Dream Map

ASKING FOR DIRECTIONS

For the Passion Question, make an appointment with the most passionate and energetic successful person you know. Before meeting with this individual, write out questions related to passion. Your goal is to learn about what makes the person tick and how she taps into her energy. Write your questions and the answers you receive in the space provided.

My Dream Map

GIVING LIFE TO THE MAP

One of the most effective ways to tap into your passion is to identify your life purpose and make sure you are aligned with it.

If you have not already done so, do some research to find a book that will help you discover your unique, God-given purpose. Many such books are on the market. As you work through the issue, attempt to write a single sentence that captures why you're here. Write that sentence below:

JOURNALING

Spend the next several days or weeks working through the passion issue. Make sure that as you reflect and write, you answer the following questions:

- [ ] In what areas of your life do you display the most initiative?
- [ ] If you could spend the rest of your life doing one thing, what would it be?
- [ ] What types of activities usually drain you of energy?
- [ ] What activities give you energy?
- [ ] What issues or causes always fire you up?
- [ ] How are your purpose, the things that give you energy, and your dream related?
- [ ] If they are not now connected, how can you work to make them connected?
- [ ] How can you incorporate more passion-producing activities into your daily schedule?
- [ ] Do you need to adjust or fine-tune your dream so that your passion, purpose, and dream are aligned?
- [ ] If you believe that you do need to make changes, what will it take for you to make them?

My Dream Map

My Dream Map

My Dream Map

My Dream Map

OBSERVATIONS AND CONCLUSIONS

What have you learned about yourself and your dream from journaling? Are your purpose, passion, and dream in alignment? If not, then you may need to revisit the Clarity Question. Do so now before moving on to the next chapters. Don't hesitate to make adjustments to your dream, so that you don't waste time creating a strategy for a dream that isn't right for you.

PLOTTING YOUR COURSE

Keeping the passion for your dream hot can be difficult. How will you do that? I recommend the following:

1. *Avoid negative people.* It's hard to stay up when you're surrounded by people who are down.
2. *Spend time with passionate people.* Many years ago, Elmer Towns, a professor and dean at Liberty University, taught me the hot poker principle. The way to get a poker hot is to put it into a fire. The way to stay passionate about your dream is to be around other people who are passionate about theirs.
3. *Use visual reminders to help you stay on track.* Put a picture related to your dream where you can see it every day.
4. *If you are a person of faith, ask God to help you stay passionate for the right things.* If God has put a dream in your heart, he will help you to complete it.

CHAPTER 5

The Pathway Question
Do I Have a Strategy to Reach My Dream?

If you've done the hard work of looking inside yourself, examining and reexamining your dream, taking ownership for it, and facing the reality of what it could take to achieve it, you're ready to think about your strategy for reaching it. Just remember that a good strategy is a starting point toward striving for your dream, but you must remain flexible as conditions change. After you create it, plan to revisit your strategy at least once a year.

YOU ARE HERE

What was your score for the pathway section of the Dream Test? That number (out of a possible 10) represents the level of effort you have put into developing a strategy for achieving your dream. Don't be concerned if the number is low when your dream is fairly new. Besides, you want to be certain that you have the right dream before you expend energy developing the strategy to reach it. But now is the time to start the process.

Think about your ability to think strategically. Has it been a strength in other areas of your life? If so, turn the page and go to the next step. If it hasn't, consider who might be able to help you with this process.

SURVEYING THE TERRAIN

When you worked through the Reality Question, you examined your starting point. In a single succinct sentence, describe where you are now in the space provided below. Next, write your dream in a single succinct sentence in the space provided below that.

Once you've done these two things, write a working strategy for bridging the gap. This will probably take you quite a bit of time. (Note: you will have to decide whether to complete this section before or after you interview someone for the "Asking for Directions" portion of this chapter on page 97.)

Your Starting Point:

_____

_____

Your Dream:

_____

_____

How to Bridge the Gap:

_____

_____

My Dream Map

My Dream Map

ASKING FOR DIRECTIONS

Of all the people you know and admire, who has the best strategic mind? Make an appointment with that person, letting him know that you would like to interview him and get his advice on your emerging strategic plan. If the person has the time, make two separate appointments so that in the first, you can ask questions about how he develops strategies before you complete "Surveying the Terrain." And in the second, you can give him your working plan and ask him to give you feedback (having used information from the first meeting to create your plan). Expect to modify your plan using his advice to improve it.

Write the questions for your interview (or interviews) here, along with the answers he provides.

My Dream Map

My Dream Map

The Pathway Question

My Dream Map

_____

_____

_____

_____

_____

_____

_____

_____

_____

_____

_____

_____

_____

_____

_____

_____

_____

_____

GIVING LIFE TO THE MAP

Look at your strategy again. If needed, revise it based on the input you received. Make sure that you write your plan as a series of specific goals, that the goals are in the right order, and that there are no gaps or missing steps in the sequence. (This may feel a little bit like you're working on a puzzle.)

Now it's time to estimate the time and the resources that will be required to accomplish each step. Write your plan in the space provided. After each step, write an expected time frame for accomplishing it and a summary of what resources will be required: money, equipment, opportunities, and so forth.

In the next two sections of this book you will be asked to examine what kind of help you'll need and whether the price you have to pay is worth it. Don't worry about assessing these two factors now. Just get down the details of your strategy here because much of the rest of your work in mapping out your dream depends on your work now. By doing this thoughtfully, you are creating the pathway toward your dream.

Step	Time	Resources

My Dream Map

Step	Time	Resources

Step	Time	Resources

My Dream Map

Step	Time	Resources

JOURNALING

Spend the next several days or weeks thinking about the strategy for achieving your dream. As you reflect and write, think about the following questions:

- ☐ Have others used the same or a similar strategy for achieving their dreams?
- ☐ Is there an out-of-the-box solution that you haven't previously considered?
- ☐ Which of the steps or goals in the plan make the most of your strengths and talents?
- ☐ Which of the steps will be the most difficult to accomplish and why?
- ☐ When you calculate the total amount of time that will be required to accomplish the dream, what is your response? Is it worth it?
- ☐ If it takes you longer than you calculated to achieve your dream, at what point would it no longer be worth pursuing?
- ☐ What resources that you currently don't possess will be difficult to acquire?
- ☐ Have you included a strategy for acquiring those resources as part of your plan?
- ☐ How will you keep yourself on track as you pursue your strategy?

My Dream Map

My Dream Map

_____

_____

_____

_____

_____

_____

_____

_____

_____

_____

_____

_____

_____

_____

_____

_____

_____

_____

My Dream Map

OBSERVATIONS AND CONCLUSIONS

What have you learned about yourself and your strategy from journaling? What details do you need to add to your strategy as a result of what you've discovered?

PLOTTING YOUR COURSE

Take the first step of your plan, break it down into specific tasks along with deadlines, and incorporate them into your calendar and to-do lists. Make the last task on the list a reminder to review your overall strategy, and then break down the next task in the same way.

CHAPTER 6

The People Question
Have I Included the People
I Need to Realize My Dream?

Poet John Donne wrote, "No man is an island, entire of itself." Our link to other people is undeniable, and the person who understands that her role in life is to help others and to be helped by others puts herself in a much better position to achieve her dream than the person who tries to go it alone.

In this section, you will be asked to examine who is already on your team, who should be on your team, and how to invite them into the process of helping you achieve your dream. That is something that must be done with integrity. That process should never be manipulative. Your goal is to find people you will help with their dreams while they help you with yours.

YOU ARE HERE

What was your score for the people section of the Dream Test? That number (out of a possible 10) gives you an indication of your starting point when it comes to the People Question. Even if your score was high, I want to encourage you to dedicate yourself to improving your team. It is impossible to have too good a group of people wanting to help you with your dream.

Make a list of the people whom you consider to be part of your team. They can be actual teammates or employees, members of your family, friends, mentors, partners—anyone who is helping you move forward in your dream. Alongside each name, write a phrase describing how that person helps you.

_____

_____

_____

_____

_____

_____

_____

_____

_____

_____

SURVEYING THE TERRAIN

Now it's time to do some analysis. First, look at your list and see whether you have people on it ahead of you who inspire you and who can help show you the way. If so, are they the right people? And are there enough of them? If not, write down others you will need.

Second, look at the strategy you wrote on pages 93–96 in response to the Pathway Question. For each step of the journey, what kinds of people will you need to help you? Give this a lot of thought. Certainly you won't be able to predict all your needs, but you want to be as thorough as you can. Create a list of people you will want according to role or contribution for each step or stage. If there are specific individuals you would like to have on your team, include their names.

Finally, make a list of encouragers and truth-tellers you would like to have on your side as you make the journey toward your dream.

ASKING FOR DIRECTIONS

Who in your profession or circle of acquaintances has put together the best team? Try to get an appointment with her. Before you meet, decide what questions to ask about her early experiences recruiting people, the way she is able to spot talent, and how she goes about communicating the vision and asking for their participation. Write your questions here.

My Dream Map

GIVING LIFE TO THE MAP

Before you try to recruit people, you must learn to communicate your dream effectively so that you can transfer the vision logically, emotionally, visually. Read a book on visionary communication to help you with that process. Then write out your vision here in such a way that it will connect with others so that you have it set in your mind. Practice communicating your vision until you can do so at any time with passion and finesse.

JOURNALING

Spend the next several days thinking through the people issue as it relates to your dream. Make sure that as you reflect and write, you answer the following questions:

- [ ] When you think about your dream, do you naturally think about the inclusion of other people?
- [ ] If not, what can you do to make yourself more people oriented?
- [ ] How could the pursuit of your dream benefit the people who might help you achieve it?
- [ ] How can you make adjustments or additions to your dream to make it more beneficial for others who help you?
- [ ] Are there people you could help with their dreams that would benefit you at the same time?
- [ ] How can you increase your network so that you have a greater pool of people to draw from?
- [ ] Who helps to support you emotionally so that you have what you need to keep going in pursuit of the dream?
- [ ] What can you do to minimize the impact of negative people on you?
- [ ] How can you make sure the pursuit of your dream is beneficial for your family?

My Dream Map

My Dream Map

My Dream Map

My Dream Map

OBSERVATIONS AND CONCLUSIONS

What have you learned about yourself, your dream, and the people issue from journaling? What, if any, modifications do you need to make to your dream or your strategy to make your dream a win for others as well as yourself?

PLOTTING YOUR COURSE

Now that you've identified who you need to help you accomplish the first goal or stage of the journey, you need to think about recruiting them. What will it take for you to get them? What obstacles currently stand in the way, and how will you remove them?

Write out your plan for finding and recruiting your team, and create deadlines for each step.

CHAPTER 7

The Cost Question
Am I Willing to Pay the Price for My Dream?

When most of us think about our dreams, we focus on the benefits. We think of all the fantastic things they will do for us and all the wonderful opportunities they will bring. That may inspire us, but it won't help us to actually move forward. To do that, we have to be willing to pay a price.

What will your dream cost you? Have you thought much about that? What are you willing to pay? Just as important, what aren't you willing to pay? Answering these questions is what this chapter is all about.

YOU ARE HERE

Your score for the cost section of the Dream Test is really a measure of your awareness that your dream will cost you as well as an indication of what you have paid so far. So if your score is low, don't let that bother you. You can improve it as long as you count the cost of your dream and make a decision to pay what will be necessary.

Take some time to reflect on what your attitude has been up to now concerning paying for your dream. And try to gauge your readiness for this next stage of the process.

SURVEYING THE TERRAIN

Review the strategy you developed for achieving your dream on pages 93–96. Every step in that process will cost you something. Go back and look at the list of people who will be needed to achieve your dreams on pages 118–19. There will be costs associated with engaging them. It's time to start assessing the costs.

For every step and every person, write down what the cost will be to you, in any and every kind of term you can think of: time, money, energy, health, resources, opportunities, and so on.

My Dream Map

The Cost Question

My Dream Map

ASKING FOR DIRECTIONS

Make an appointment to interview someone you admire who is ahead of you in your career field or area of interest. Your task this time is very straightforward. Ask him what he had to give up in order to achieve what he has, and ask him what he thinks you will have to pay in order to achieve your dream. Take notes in the space provided.

My Dream Map

GIVING LIFE TO THE MAP

Think about the four or five people you most admire. They can be acquaintances, public figures, or individuals from history. What did it cost them to achieve their dreams? If you are unsure, do research on them. Do you see any common threads among their sacrifices? Do you see any similarities between their journey and yours? Record your observations here.

JOURNALING

Spend the next several days or weeks wrestling through the cost issue. Make sure that as you reflect and write, you answer the following questions:

- [ ] How much are you willing to pay for your dream?
- [ ] In addition to what you have already been told by others and what you yourself have identified as costs, what *else* would you be willing to give up to accomplish your dream?
- [ ] What are you *not* willing to pay in order to achieve your dream?
- [ ] Are you willing to start paying the price *now*?
- [ ] How long are you willing to keep paying for your dream?
- [ ] What price should others around you expect to pay for your dream?
- [ ] Have you talked to them about that price, and are they willing to pay it?
- [ ] How willing are you to face criticism from others as you pursue your dream?
- [ ] How will you respond if the price to achieve your dream gets too high?
- [ ] What would the fallout be to those closest to you if the price got to be too high and you had to abandon the quest for your dream?
- [ ] Once you have achieved your dream, what are you willing to pay to keep it?

My Dream Map

My Dream Map

The Cost Question

My Dream Map

My Dream Map

OBSERVATIONS AND CONCLUSIONS

What have you learned about yourself and your dream, and what conclusions have you drawn? Write them here.

PLOTTING YOUR COURSE

Thinking about your next stage of strategy, the people needed, and the costs, write out an action plan for paying the price. (And schedule a time and process so that you can do this for subsequent stages or goals.)

CHAPTER 8

The Tenacity Question
Am I Moving Closer to My Dream?

Calvin Coolidge asserted, "Nothing in the world can take the place of persistence. Talent will not; nothing is more common than unsuccessful men with talent. Genius will not; unrewarded genius is almost a proverb. Education will not; the world is full of educated derelicts. Persistence and determination alone are omnipotent. The slogan 'press on' has solved, and always will solve, the problems of the human race."

Do you have the mind-set described by the thirtieth president of the United States? Do you have the will to press on? I hope you do, because if you lack tenacity, all the work you've already done toward achieving your dream could be for naught. Don't fall short of your dream because you lack the will to pursue it. Do what you must to press on.

YOU ARE HERE

If you took the Dream Test before beginning the process of working through this book, there is a good chance that your score in the tenacity section could have already improved. Before you go back to see what your score was, retake that section of the test now. (Remember how to score them: No = 0, Somewhat = 1, and Yes = 2.)

A. I can identify obstacles I have already overcome in the pursuit of my dream.

B. I possess an attitude of initiative related to my dream, and I am unafraid of taking bold steps to take me closer to my dream.

C. I do something every day—even if it's very small—to move closer to my dream.

D. I expect to do extraordinarily difficult things to grow and change so that I can accomplish my dream, and I have prepared myself mentally to do them.

E. I refuse to take no for an answer when it comes to my dream.

Tally your current score and compare it to your previous one. If your score has improved, you have already grown. Congratulations! In particular, I want you to look at whether you improved for C: I do something every day—even if it's very small—to move closer to my dream. If you didn't score a 2, you may already be thinking and learning about your dream, but you're not yet *doing* enough for it.

SURVEYING THE TERRAIN

If you don't take action to move closer to accomplishing your dream as much as you should or would like to, then you need to figure out why. Spend some time brainstorming every possible reason you can think of to explain why people fail to act on something they say is important to them. Do that in the space provided.

ASKING FOR DIRECTIONS

Who are the most tenacious people you know? They refuse to ever give up on anything important to them. They overcome incredible odds. Think of the two to four who best exhibit that quality. Invite them to dinner or lunch to talk about how they get things done and the fire that burns inside them. Plan to throw out a question or two to get them talking about it, then take notes and ask follow-up questions.

My Dream Map

GIVING LIFE TO THE MAP

Read one or more biographies of people who overcame incredible odds to accomplish something important to them. Record important observations here.

JOURNALING

Spend the next several days or weeks wrestling through the tenacity issue. Make sure that as you reflect and write, you answer the following questions:

- ☐ Are you naturally more a doer or a thinker? (Hint: if the Pathway Question was incredibly easy for you, you are probably more of a thinker.)
- ☐ If you tend toward thinking, what can you do to make yourself more proactive?
- ☐ Does the desire for perfection ever keep you from taking action?
- ☐ If so, what can you do to overcome that hindrance?
- ☐ What action can you take every day to put yourself into a more activistic state of mind?
- ☐ Are there activistic people in your life with whom you could partner to get more done?
- ☐ Which is more appealing to you: a bold action that takes you a major step forward or many small daily actions that chip away at a goal?
- ☐ How can you tap into that?
- ☐ What aspect of your dream really fires you up?
- ☐ How can you harness that enthusiasm to make you more tenacious?

My Dream Map

My Dream Map

My Dream Map

My Dream Map

OBSERVATIONS AND CONCLUSIONS

What have you learned about yourself, your dream, and the tenacity issue from journaling?

PLOTTING YOUR COURSE

Take some time to write a tenacity manifesto for yourself in the space provided. Make a copy of it and post it someplace where you will see it every day. Then make a commitment to do something every day—no matter how small—that brings you closer to your dream.

CHAPTER 9

The Fulfillment Question
Does Working Toward My Dream Bring Satisfaction?

Is it worth pursuing a dream that makes you miserable in the process? I don't believe it is. I'm convinced that purpose and fulfillment go together. God doesn't make mistakes. What you have been created to do, what gives you satisfaction, and what you dream about should all line up. If they don't, you've missed something in the process of pursuing your dream.

This chapter is really about affirming that you truly are pursuing the right dream. If at the end of this section of the book you reach the conclusion that you don't gain fulfillment from working toward your stated dream, you need to have the courage to go back and start the whole process over again, beginning with the Ownership Question. That would be wiser than spending even one more day chasing after the wrong dream!

YOU ARE HERE

What was your score for the fulfillment section of the Dream Test? If it was a 9 or 10, then turn the page. If it wasn't, retake this slightly modified version now to see whether the work you've done in the previous chapters and adjustments you've made to your thinking have changed your score. (Score your answers as follows: No = 0, Somewhat = 1, and Yes = 2.)

    A. I am willing to give up my idealism in order to make my dream become reality.

    B. I understand that the pursuit of any significant dream leads one into a difficult learning curve, and I am ready to face it.

    C. I am ready and willing to work for years or even decades to achieve my dream because it is that important to me.

    D. I am willing to make discoveries about myself a goal "on the way" to my dream because I know that will help sustain me.

    E. I enjoy the pursuit of my dream so much that even if I fail, I will consider my life to have been well spent.

How do your two scores compare? (Questions B and D in this version are phrased to indicate a *willingness* to gain fulfillment from growth; in the original version, they indicated an *intentionality* to gain fulfillment from growth.) What does the difference in your scores, if any, tell you about yourself? Record your observation here.

SURVEYING THE TERRAIN

In the space provided, make a list of the things in life that give you the greatest fulfillment. After you complete the list, consider how you can connect those favorite activities to the pursuit of your dream.

ASKING FOR DIRECTIONS

Make an appointment with a successful person you admire who seems to be highly contented in his work. Plan to ask questions related to how fulfilling that person's work is and how he has dealt with the aspects of his career that have not brought fulfillment. Write your questions and notes here.

My Dream Map

GIVING LIFE TO THE MAP

Is fulfillment solely a function of having the right dream? Or is it also largely dependent on a person's attitude?

Devote some time to considering the role that attitude plays in fulfillment. Assess your attitude, and write about specific ways you can improve your attitude and make the pursuit more enjoyable.

JOURNALING

Spend the next several days or weeks reflecting and writing about the fulfillment issue. As you do, answer the following questions:

- ☐ Which is more important to you: the journey or the destination?
- ☐ What is your attitude toward the length of time your dream is likely to take?
- ☐ What kinds of things can you do to keep yourself fulfilled while living in the gap between the birth of your dream and its realization?
- ☐ What role does your growth as a person play in your sense of fulfillment while you are pursuing your dream?
- ☐ If it should play a greater role, what changes must you make in your life to make that adjustment?
- ☐ Does the pursuit of your dream cause you to discover and accomplish other small dreams along the way?
- ☐ What do you do to celebrate the incremental advances you are making along the way?
- ☐ What part does failure play in achieving success?
- ☐ How are you at dealing with your mistakes and shortcomings?
- ☐ In the past, have you been too idealistic?
- ☐ If so, what adjustments to your thinking can you make to help yourself?

My Dream Map

My Dream Map

My Dream Map

My Dream Map

OBSERVATIONS AND CONCLUSIONS

What have you learned about yourself and your dream from journaling?

PLOTTING YOUR COURSE

Once again assess your level of fulfillment for the pursuit of your dream. If it is still too low to sustain you for the long haul, talk to three people close to you about the problem. Ask them to help you recognize whether the issue is one of the following:

1. The wrong dream
2. A poor attitude
3. Unrealistic expectations
4. Emotional immaturity
5. A violation of your values

Then ask them to help you figure out an action plan to address the issue. Write that action plan here.

My Dream Map

CHAPTER 10

The Significance Question
Does My Dream Benefit Others?

Is it possible for people to have a dream worthy of their efforts if it does not benefit anyone but them? Ultimately, I believe the answer is no. To have a dream worth dedicating your life to, you must answer yes to the Significance Question.

In this final section of the book, you'll be asked to think about the impact that your dream will have on others. I believe that just about every dream has the potential to be expanded so that it benefits others. Your job here is to find a way to do that.

YOU ARE HERE

What was your score for the significance section of the Dream Test? That number (out of a possible 10) represents the current level of significance for your dream. What is your reaction to that? Take some time to reflect on it and write about what it means as your starting point.

_____

_____

_____

_____

_____

_____

_____

_____

_____

_____

_____

_____

SURVEYING THE TERRAIN

When you defined your dream and wrote it out, how much emphasis was on benefiting others? Was the focus on personal achievement and success? Or was service to others a major part of it? Be honest in your assessment. Record your observations here.

_____

_____

_____

_____

_____

_____

_____

_____

_____

_____

_____

_____

ASKING FOR DIRECTIONS

For this final interview regarding the Significance Question, make an appointment with the person you know who has added the most value to other people or made the most significant contribution to others. Learn what got her started on the pathway toward helping others. Discover how that relates to her dreams. Ask what her most significant accomplishment has been so far. Find out what keeps her going.

Write your questions prior to your meeting, and write your notes here.

My Dream Map

GIVING LIFE TO THE MAP

Imagine yourself watching your funeral, listening to your eulogy. What would you want people to say about you? Imagine the boldest, most significant and rewarding life possible for yourself. Write that eulogy here.

JOURNALING

Spend the next several days or weeks wrestling through the significance issue. As you reflect and write, make sure that you answer the following questions:

- ☐ Why do you want to accomplish this dream?
- ☐ Does your dream reflect a desire in you for survival, success, or significance?
- ☐ Will the fulfillment of your dream have a direct benefit for others? If so, how?
- ☐ Will the pursuit of your dream benefit the people who help you to accomplish it? If so, how?
- ☐ How can you shift or expand your dream so that it significantly benefits others and not just yourself?
- ☐ How will the accomplishment of your dream matter in five, ten, or fifty years?
- ☐ How can you make your dream have a longer lasting impact?
- ☐ How is your dream part of a cause greater than yourself?
- ☐ What would happen to others if you were unable to achieve your dream?

My Dream Map

My Dream Map

My Dream Map

My Dream Map

OBSERVATIONS AND CONCLUSIONS

What have you learned about yourself, your dream, and the significance issue from journaling?

PLOTTING YOUR COURSE

Write out your dream one more time, paying particular attention to include the positive impact that it will have on either the people who work with you to accomplish it or the people who will benefit from it directly as recipients of the dream.

CONCLUSION

My hope and prayer are that *My Dream Map* has helped you to reflect, discover, and evaluate your dream more deeply than you ever could have on your own. And I trust that you can now answer a resounding yes to each of the ten dream questions.

I hope that this process has added value to you. However, there's one more thing I want to tell you. You're not yet finished with your dream. Though you may now have an excellent handle on your dream, and though your general course may be set, you should not expect your dream to remain static. As you learn, grow, and change, so will your dream. That's why I've included extra pages after this conclusion for you to continue taking notes as your dream evolves. I recommend that you keep this book near you and use it as a reference as you pursue your dream.

May God bless you, and may your dream bless others.

ABOUT THE AUTHOR

John C. Maxwell is an internationally recognized leadership expert, speaker, and author who has sold more than 16 million books. His organizations have trained more than 2 million leaders worldwide. Dr. Maxwell is the founder of EQUIP and INJOY Stewardship Services. Every year he speaks to Fortune 500 companies, international government leaders, and audiences as diverse as the United States Military Academy at West Point, the National Football League, and ambassadors at the United Nations. A *New York Times, Wall Street Journal,* and *Business Week* best-selling author, Maxwell was named the World's Top Leadership Guru by Leadershipgurus.net. He was also one of only twenty-five authors and artists named to Amazon.com's 10th Anniversary Hall of Fame. Three of his books, *The 21 Irrefutable Laws of Leadership, Developing the Leader Within You,* and *The 21 Indispensable Qualities of a Leader,* have each sold more than a million copies.